May you rejoice as you

celebrate your birthday!

This blessing, *May You Rejoice*, originally appeared in *Out of the Ordinary: Prayers, Poems, and Reflections for Every Season* by Joyce Rupp. Copyright ©2000 by Joyce Rupp.

© 2010 by Joyce Rupp

Founded in 1865, Ave Maria Press is a ministry of the United States Province of Holy Cross.

www.avemariapress.com

ISBN-10 1-59471-257-3   ISBN-13 978-1-59471-257-9

Cover image © Superstock. Interior images © iStockphoto.

Cover and text design by Katherine Robinson Coleman.

Printed and bound in the United States of America.

May you rejoice

a blessing for your birthday

Joyce Rupp

*G*od will rejoice over you with happy song. God will dance with shouts of joy for you as on a day of festival.

~ Zephaniah 3:28

*M*ay you sip
contentedly from the
fragrant wine of your life.

*M*ay you stretch

eagerly into the opening light

of each new day.

May you discover

kernels of wisdom hidden

in unwanted experiences.

May you find

comfort and consolation

when you are hurting.

May you know the

protection and guidance

of your angels.

*M*ay you hear

the tender voice of the Beloved

calling to you in the deepest

part of your being.

*M*ay you have
a soul friend whose
unconditional love gives you
courage to keep growing.

May you be a bearer
of loving kindness when you
meet those who suffer.

May you gather your

daily blessings to your heart

and relish their presence.

May you never give up seeking greater peace for yourself and for your world.

May you go to sleep

each evening aware of being held

in the embrace of a merciful

and welcoming God.

May you hear the
marvelous music singing in
your soul every moment,
lauding the exquisite
gift of being alive.

May you rejoice as you celebrate your birthday!

ISBN-13: 978-1-59471-257-9
ISBN-10: 1-59471-257-3

AVE MARIA PRESS
Notre Dame, IN
www.avemariapress.com
A Ministry of the United States Province of Holy Cross